WALKS w

in the
AROUND WINDERMERE

Dennis and Jan Kelsall

A Questa Guide

© Dennis and Jan Kelsall, 2000
ISBN 1 898808 07 4

ADVICE TO READERS

Readers are advised that while the author had made every effort to
ensure the accuracy of this guidebook, and has been required to
revisit all the routes during the course of preparing the book,
changes can occur which may affect the contents. The Publishers
would welcome notes of any changes you find.

Also by Dennis and Jan Kelsall
Walks with Children in the Lake District:
Ambleside and Grasmere
Around Kendal

Published by
Questa Publishing, 27 Camwood, Bamber Bridge, Preston, Lancashire
PR5 8LA
and printed by
Carnmor Print, 95/97 London Road, Preston, Lancashire, PR1 4BA

Contents

Introduction

Cleaving a path inland from the mosses that once bordered the northern shores of Morecambe Bay, the valley of Windermere neatly divides the hills that form the southern outliers to Lakeland's central peaks. Often abruptly rising out of the surrounding agricultural countryside, their contours are invariably softened by a rich sylvan cloak, which provides a verdant beauty often absent from the higher landscapes of Cumbria's heartland. But the trees are not everywhere, and in the south-western quadrant particularly, gently rolling plateaux reveal expansive panoramic scenes that extend from the coast across to the distant Pennine hills in the east.

The first mention of the lake itself in literary verse appears to have been in 1636 by Richard Braithwaite, in a poem that mourned the loss of forty-seven souls crossing to the eastern bank after attending the celebrations of a wedding in Hawkshead.

> O Windermere, who art renown'd afarre
> For thy sole-breeding there unvalued charre,
> And with thy spatious channell doest divide
> Two ancient Counties seated side by side

Although still renowned afar, other things have changed. The 'charre', a fish related to the trout, has since become a delicacy and albeit now entirely in Cumbria, the shores of the lake did indeed once separate two counties; Lancashire, to the south and west, from Westmorland, to the north and east. This might appear incongruous to younger generations, but in the centuries that preceded the railways, this southern corner of what we now call Lakeland, was more readily accessible from the rest of the country across the sands of Morecambe Bay, despite the dangers that the crossing presented. Therefore, although the lake itself was once encapsulated within the borders of Westmorland, the majority of the walks described in this book tread the pathways of old Lancashire. This distinction is perhaps still relevant, since visitors often ignore much of the area. Intent on the better-known attractions of the higher hills and mountains, some dismiss this corner as not really being part of the 'Lakes'.

Yet this is not to say that the landscape here is any the less rewarding. Indeed, in many respects it is infinitely more varied, it being possible to visit woodland, lakeside, stream banks, pasture, moorland and valley, all within a single walk. It has other advantages too in that the terrain is somewhat less demanding and, despite in some places giving an appearance of utter remoteness, you are never that far from 'civilisation'. Furthermore, the lower altitude brings with it a gentler weather pattern that often leaves these walks safely attainable when expeditions to the higher fells might be considered foolhardy for all but the highly experienced.

Even so, there is a sense of excitement and adventure to be had here, in exploring an area that is equally as rich in its past as it is in its present. As you walk along the quiet paths and byways you might find it hard to believe that, well into the twentieth century, there was considerable industry carried out in the surrounding woods and valleys. Besides the active management of the forests by coppicing, thinning, bark stripping and felling, there were charcoal burners, iron smelters, tanners and lime burners carrying out their trades in countless small glades hidden amongst the trees. Streams and small reservoirs powered an assortment of mills that undertook sawing, turnery, metal forging and textile production. But as the industrial revolution gathered momentum, improved transport links, increasing mechanisation and industrial centralisation brought an end to these traditional mainstays of the local economy. Of course, farming and sheep rearing continue, but they now support far fewer people than they did even fifty years ago. The climate and lie of the countryside does not lend itself to many of the modern agricultural techniques and competition from elsewhere and the development of man-made fabrics has decimated a woollen industry that brought a considerable wealth to the area throughout the medieval period. In all but a few places, virtually all trace of these activities has disappeared, but clues remain in now-ruinous buildings, abandoned weirs and leats, old trackways and sometimes equally as tangible, the place-names marked on your map.

It is not only the past, however, that instils a wider interest to these walks, the variety of wildlife and plants in the area can provide so many diversions and investigatory halts that a short stroll can end up taking all day to complete. The proximity of the coast and sheltering protection of trees and valleys foster environments in which you will find a host of flowers and plants. There will be surprises at any time of the year, but the flowers of spring and early summer are a particular delight. Carry with you a pair of binoculars, for the woods and heaths harbour a rich assortment of birds. There are mammals too, and although most, like badgers and small rodents, remain well hidden during the day, you will spot rabbits and, if you are quiet, perhaps a deer or two. Whilst foxes are also common, you are more likely to smell their passing rather than meet them face to face.

Designed to be reasonably within the capacity of most people, none of the walks in this collection is overly demanding. That is not to say that there are not some steep ascents, but they are generally short and you will always be able to find some distraction, a flower or a view, to justify a brief pause. The walks vary in distance, but no indication is given of the time required to complete them since this depends on your own approach.

You might like to take with you on the walks a field guide to help identify the plants and birds you will find along the way. The small plans in the book are no substitute for a detailed map and, even if it is not always necessary in order to identify the correct route, you will find that a map can add immensely to your enjoyment of the day, helping to identify distant views or suggesting your own personal variations to the course suggested in the text.

1

Wansfell Pike from Troutbeck

Despite its relatively low elevation at 484 metres, Wansfell offers marvellous views across Windermere and its surrounding countryside. If approached from Ambleside, there is a steep pull to the top, but this walk from Troutbeck is more gradual and the return walk around the hill's southern flank is a pleasure not to be missed.

Total distance: 6.5 miles (10.5km)
Height gain: 1,850 feet (563m)
Start: Troutbeck Church on the A592 road from Windermere to Kirkstone. GR NY412027

1   Begin along a track beside the churchyard, leaving the main road immediately north of the church. A short way along, go right over a waymarked stile and walk ahead to the top of the field. Keep going through a series of gates, initially paralleling a beck that flows at the base of a cleft below. On reaching a junction of tracks, turn left towards Troutbeck and, where the way then forks, bear right, shortly to emerge onto a lane through the village.

During the medieval period, the peace of this northern corner of England was often disrupted by bands marauding Scots, sweeping from the Borders to plunder isolated farms and villages. But for a time, this valley had a champion in Hugh Hird, a giant of a man who single-handedly drove back a party of raiders. However, he had settled here as a squatter and when he similarly treated the rightful tenant who came to take up his property, Hird was summoned before the king to explain his behaviour. Impressed by his strength and the way he had dealt with the Scots, the king granted Hird his cottage with some land to farm and he returned to live out his life in the valley.

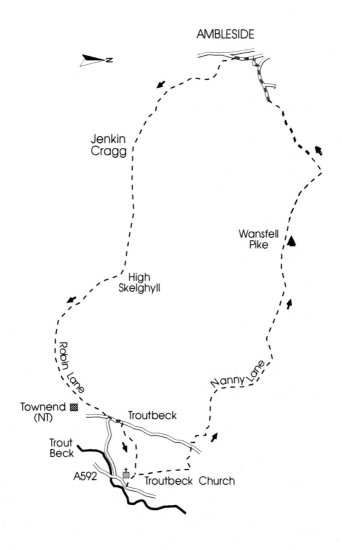

N

AMBLESIDE

Jenkin
Cragg

Wansfell
Pike

High
Skelghyll

Robin Lane

Nanny Lane

Townend ▨
(NT)

Troutbeck

Trout
Beck

A592

Troutbeck Church

2   Go left, but almost immediately, turn right into Lane Foot Farm from where a track, marked Nanny Lane on the map, climbs the hillside behind. Although initially a steep pull, after passing through a gate the gradient eases. After about ¾ mile, where the track bends to the right, pass through a kissing-gate in the wall on the left, from which a clear, rising path, signed to Ambleside via Wansfell, meanders across the open moorland. After passing through another gate higher up, carry on towards Wansfell's summit, which now dominates the view ahead.

The summit, marked by a trig point, affords a spectacular view along the lake to distant Morecambe Bay and the sea beyond. Below your feet, contained by the steep sides of the narrow valley is Ambleside, which from here appears almost toy-like. If you look above the head of the lake, you will see the site of a Roman fort, Galava. It was established under Agricola, who came to Britain as Governor in the year 78 and led a campaign to extend the Roman occupation north, reaching the Firth of Forth.

3   Walk ahead across the top and follow a clear path dropping steeply down Wansfell's western flank towards Ambleside. Eventually, the path joins the course of a stream and descends to a wall. From there, an old enclosed lane leads gently more downwards to the left, taking you towards the town.

4   Approaching Ambleside, after the track becomes metalled, turn into the first street on the left. At the bottom of that, turn right and, then go left again at the end onto Old Lake Road. Walk on towards the main road, but just before you get there, turn left onto a track signed to Jenkin Crag, Skelghyll and Troutbeck.

5   Climb up to a fork, and there bear right to Jenkin Crag. The track now runs more level, giving a view across the head of the lake before entering Skelghyll Wood. Keep to the main track, which shortly climbs and bends across a stream. Higher up, after the gradient eases again, you will pass Jenkin Crag, where there is a fine view across Windermere. To enjoy it, follow a narrow path through a gap in the wall on the right.

6   Return to the track and continue as before, shortly emerging from the wood towards a farm, High Skelghyll. Beyond the farmyard, carry on along a tarmac track and where it then forks, bear left, dropping to cross a stream. Just beyond, go through a handgate on the left, from where a path is signed to Troutbeck.

7   Rising across an open hillside, the way passes a ruined barn and then fords a stream to join a crossing track, Hundreds Road, where you should turn right. Now, with all the climbing behind you and the prospect of a pleasant walk to Troutbeck, you can confidently stride out. Further on, ignore a path signed off to the right and bear left along the main track (here marked Robin Lane on the map), eventually to emerge onto a lane in the village by the post office.

Owing to the valley's relative isolation, the feudal system imposed after the Norman invasion had less effect here than in most other areas of the country and throughout the Middle Ages the farmers retained considerable freedoms under their manorial overlords. Importantly, holdings remained in the same family from generation to generation and there was thus no disincentive to a man improving his property. By the seventeenth century, prosperity from wool production fuelled a spate of rebuilding and many of the village's dwellings date from that period. The National Trust now owns one of them, Townend, and you will find it just along the lane to the right of the junction.

8   Follow the lane to the left through Troutbeck for about 150 yards, until you reach High Fold Farm on your right. Turn into its drive, signed as a bridleway to the church, and walk past the buildings and on along an enclosed track. At the bottom keep ahead through a gate and over a stream to return to the main road by the church.

The little church here is thought to date from at least the beginning of the sixteenth century, although several rebuildings and refurbishments have taken place over the years. One of its interesting later features is the east window, which was designed by Edward Burne Jones and made by the William Morris Company.

9

2

Orrest Head and Allen Knott

Only a short walk out of Windermere, Orrest Head is one of those delightful locations from which the breadth of its view is totally unexpected and far exceeds any expectations. The route continues across the rolling countryside to the north, skirting the foot of Allen Knott before eventually returning below Orrest Head.

Total distance: 4.5 miles (7.5km)
Height gain: 880 feet (268m)
Start: A591 in Windermere, by the Windermere Hotel. GR SD413987

1   Immediately west of the Windermere Hotel and opposite the National Westminster Bank, a waymarked drive to Orrest Head climbs northwards from the main road. Beyond Elleray Wood Cottage, it continues as a woodland track, shortly reaching a fork. There, bear right, ascending through the trees to a lateral track at the top. Now turn right, and at the end of the track, go left through a kissing-gate and walk up to the top of Orrest Head.

2   Continue in the same direction across the summit, following a descending path towards some conspicuous white buildings in the middle distance, Causeway Farm. After crossing a stile part way down the hill, continue parallel to a wall that runs over to the left, eventually joining a field track, which ends at a gate and stile leading out onto a lane.

3   Turn right, but in less than ¼ mile, just before reaching Near Orrest Farm, climb a wall stile on the left, waymarked to Far Orrest. Follow the field edge around the farm outbuildings to a kissing-gate and then on across a small meadow to a second kissing-gate in its far corner. The way continues at the edge of a small copse

and, over a stile, back into an open field. Walk across it to climb another stile at an indented corner opposite and then follow the right-hand wall away. Beyond a ladder stile in the next corner and then immediately over a stream, bear right towards some buildings that mark Far Orrest. After crossing another ladder stile, a field track leads the way to a gate out of the fields by the farm.

4   Go though a kissing-gate directly opposite and bear left around the perimeter of the farm. Just beyond the buildings, go through another kissing-gate and turn right, leaving the farm along an old walled track. Through a gate at its far end, follow a wall on the left past the foot of Allen Knott and keep going in the same direction through a gate opening across the next field, finally emerging onto a lane.

Hill forts

When the Romans reached this remote corner of the country during the first century, they found the land to be already occupied by native tribes. Living in small groups, they had settled above rather than within the valleys, building small settlements that could be defended both from wild animals and other clans. There is one such site here, above the path on the top of Allen Knott, a small rectangular enclosure that has been identified as an Iron Age hill fort. Although scant remains often make them difficult to date, many are thought to have been occupied from about 300 BC and may well have continued in use after the Romans left the area.

5   Turn left and then left again at a junction a short way down to reach a drive on the left, waymarked to Far Orrest. Follow that past some cottages to a fork and bear left again, to return to Far Orrest, about ¼ mile distant.

6   Approaching the farm, bear left to pass in front of buildings, but then as you reach a pair of gates, leave the drive to go over a stile on the right. Walk to a waymarked gate and through to the fields beyond. A track then guides you across successive fields, finally emerging past a cottage onto a lane by Crosses Farm. Turn left and walk towards Causeway Farm, about ¼ mile away.

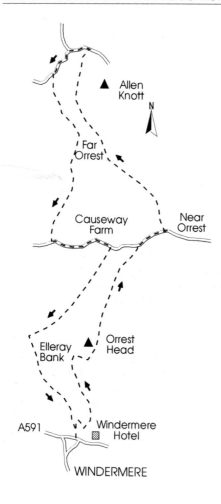

7 Opposite the farm entrance, turn right through a gate onto a wide enclosed track into an open field. Follow it ahead, but when the track later turns left towards the higher ground, leave it and continue on by the right-hand wall to a stile in the field corner. Over that, walk forwards and cross another stile, now following the edge of a wood. After cresting a rise, drop to the bottom corner of the field, where a stile takes the path into the wood. Go down through the trees to a path at the bottom and turn left.

8 Shortly, the path joins a drive by Elleray Bank. Follow it to the right, but then, almost immediately, leave it on the left for a continuation of the earlier path. When you reach houses a little further on, stay with the path ahead, which follows the foot of a wooded bank behind the buildings. It will eventually emerge onto the drive along which the walk began, there turn right, and walk back down to Windermere.

3

Around Rulbuts Hill

*Although easily accessible from the main routes to
Windermere, the lovely countryside above the eastern
shores of the lake is seldom visited and can be devoid of
people, even on a busy bank holiday. This undemanding
walk across rolling farmland and gentle fellside pastures
is a chance to explore some of these lesser-known
corners.*

Total distance: 4.5 miles (7km)
Height gain: 360 feet (110m)
**Start: There is roadside parking on Ghyll Head Road
by Ghyll Head Reservoir, from where the walk
begins. GR SD398924**

1   Towards the northern end of Ghyll Head Reservoir and on the
opposite side of the lane, two adjacent tall gates lead onto the
hillside. Go through the right most of them, from which a path is
signed to Black Beck, Rosthwaite and Winster. Before you reach
a second gate, just ahead, turn right onto a grass track and walk
away, initially beside the SSSI of Candlestick Moss, which lies over
the fence on the left. Keep to the main path across a sparsely
wooded open heath, later passing through a fence by a handgate,
beyond which the hillside has been planted with young trees.

Buzzards
*Keep your eyes open and you may see a buzzard, patrolling the
hillside or perched in a tree. Although quite a bit smaller than the
golden eagle, they are one of the largest birds of prey you will
see in Britain and are unmistakable in their size and shape.
Gliding above the rocks or soaring high into the sky, their flight
appears effortless, and even taking off from a tree or the top of
a telegraph post, they display the same air of gracefulness. For*

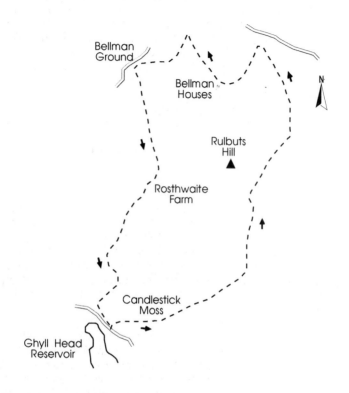

* food, they will kill rabbits or small mammals, but also take birds,
* frogs, carrion and even insects.

2 After about ½ mile you will come to a crossing track beside a
stone wall. Ignore the stile ahead and instead, turn left to follow the
track. Shortly, after passing through a gate/stile, the way begins to
lose height and a fine panorama opens up across the valley.
Continue ahead where the way is later joined by another track from
the left and lower down, walk past gates, first two on the right and
then one on the left, before reaching a final one at the bottom.
Beyond that, continue through an old wood, leaving by another
gate further on.

3   Back on open heath and then pasture, the route follows a wall on the right, passing through a couple of openings and eventually reaching a shallow corner in the field. Ignore a walled track on the right at that point leading out to the road, instead bear left, following the continuation of the wall, rising along the edge of the field. A track later develops, which through a gate, carries on around to the right to a farm, Bellman Houses.

4   Walk through the farmyard and out along a track at the far side past a caravan site. Beyond there, pass out by a gate and continue down towards the bottom of an open field. There, leave the track and turn left, following a wall on your right-hand side beside a couple of fields to the next farm, Bellman Ground.

5   As you approach the buildings, turn left onto a tarmac drive and follow it for almost ½ mile over a hill to Rosthwaite Farm. Approaching its entrance gates, bear left and follow the drive around the perimeter of the buildings and gardens, passing out through a couple of gates on the far side. The way now degrades to a stone track and leads away across an open fell pasture. Keep ahead where a footpath joins from the right and you will you shortly reach a solitary oak. There, turn left onto a grass track signed to Ghyll Head.

6   After climbing a stile over the wall ahead, carry on beside a fence on the right to a kissing-gate. Immediately through that, turn right through another gate into a National Park Access Area. A winding path leads across a wooded bracken heath, shortly dropping to the lane at Ghyll Head Reservoir, where the walk began.

4

Fell Foot Brow to Cartmel Fell

*Although there is little obvious ascent during this walk,
the open, rolling topography through which it passes
affords some magnificent views along the Winster valley
and gives a fine sense of achievement for relatively little
effort.*

Total distance: 5.3 miles (8.5km)
(Gummer's How 1.2 miles (2km))
Height gain: 660 feet (200m)
(Gummer's How 400 feet (120m)
Start: Car park below Gummer's How. GR SD389876

1   From the car park, walk up the road to the right for about 500
yards to a junction where the trees on the right end. There, turn
right onto Sow How Lane and walk down to the farm at its end.
Keep going ahead through the farmyard to leave along a track that
continues onto the fell beyond.

2   About 100 yards after the farm, turn left onto a marked
bridleway that crosses a pasture towards a reservoir, Sow How
Tarn, which is partly screened by a copse of trees. Keep going
below its low dam and cross an outflow stream before rising to
pass through a gap in a wall. The way, now more level, continues
to a gate that leads into a wood. After gently descending through
the trees, the track emerges onto a pasture and follows its lower
wall. At the bottom, turn sharply right and drop down to an
abandoned farmhouse, marked Heights Cottage on your map.

Heights Cottage
*The old farmhouse is in a derelict condition and you should not
go inside. However, from outside you can see that the living
arrangements for the farmer and his family were set side by*

side with the barns used for storage, fodder and the animals. The self-contained arrangement was convenient in several ways; it allowed easy access for feeding the stock which was over-wintered in the barn and who, in turn, provided some heat to the living quarters next door.

3   Turn left to go past the building and follow a track down beside a wall to the bottom of the field and out through a gate onto the rising open fell beyond. A green track continues ahead over a low hump before dipping past a marshy area. About 20 yards beyond there, leave the obvious track, which curves away to the right, turning left onto an indistinct trod that climbs past a clump of rocks. On the other side of those, the way then levels and an obvious track develops that leads gently down the far side of the hill, eventually ending at a gate. Through that, turn right and walk out to a lane at the bottom.

4   Go right and follow the lane for about 250 yards to a fork. There, leave the metalled way, going left onto a path at the edge of a wood, following a wall down to a stile leading into St Anthony's church-yard at Cartmel Fell.

St Anthony's Church

The church is a lovely old building in a beautiful setting, surrounded by an old graveyard, whose ancient stones lean as if to emphasise their age but which are somehow rejuvenated each spring by the multitude of crocuses and daffodils that burst through the carpet of soft grass and moss between them. The chapel was built in 1504 as a chapel-of-ease to save the villagers having to walk all the way to the parish church at Cartmel for Sunday service and communion. However, it was not until 1712 that baptisms, marriages and funerals could be conducted here.

Inside is a seventeenth-century 'three-decker' pulpit, now comparatively rare in our churches since most were swept away during the Victorian zeal for 'restoration'. The pew at the base was for the parish clerk, who was expected to lead the congregation in the responses and singing, whilst the reading desk above was where the lessons and prayers were delivered. The preaching pulpit at the top gave the vicar a commanding

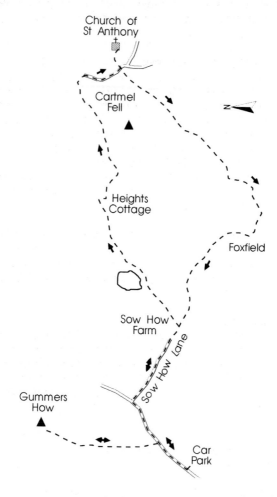

view over his flock whilst he delivered his sermon. Behind, there are two wonderful box pews, one of which served during the week as the village school until a separate schoolhouse was built in 1872. It appears that the children did not always give

their full attention, for carved on the bench is the outline of a
playing board for pachisi, an Indian game from which our own
ludo was derived.

5   Retrace your steps, climbing back to the lane by the fork and cross to a ladder stile spanning a wall directly opposite. From there, a path climbs the fellside, curving left to a second wall stile. Over that, walk away along a green track across a sparsely wooded and bracken-cloaked slope that shortly leads to an enclosed wood. Keep going through that and on, gently losing height across more open heath beyond its far side. Continue ahead where a path joins from the left and, after crossing a stream, the way will lead you to the bottom of a short contained track. At the top of that, go left onto a farm track and, ultimately, emerge through a gate onto a tarmac track.

6   Now turn right and walk up to some cottages at Foxfield. Beyond there, the way continues as an unsurfaced track, undulating across an open fell. It is about ½ mile or so back to Sow How Farm, where you will rejoin your outward track. Walk back along the lanes to the car park.

Gummer's How

Across the road from the car park rises Gummer's How and you
may like to end the day with the short climb to its summit, from
which there is a splendid view over Windermere to the distant
mountains in the west. Quite obvious to the north-west is
Coniston Old Man, and to its right, peeping from behind lesser
heights, you can just see Scafell Pike.

7   The top of Gummer's How is clearly visible from the car park and the footpath to it leaves the road on the left, just a little way along up the hill.

8   After enjoying the magnificent view from its summit, just turn around and walk back to the car park.

5

South of Backbarrow

The country below the bottom end of Windermere rises steeply out of the Leven valley to a hillocky plateau that falls more gently to the east. Although it can sometimes be wet underfoot, the area is fine walking country and gives a wonderful sense of remoteness. During the first part of the walk, some of the paths are not obvious and, particularly if it is misty, you will find your compass very useful.

Total distance: 6.2 miles (10km) 🐾
Height Gain: 720 feet (220m)
Start: Pull-in beside a wireless transmitter above Low Brow Edge, about ½ mile south of Backbarrow.
GR SD358841

1   Opposite the pull-in and heading north-east from the road, a track, marked as a bridleway, follows the edge of a rough pasture to a gap in a crossing fence. About 100 yards further on, where the track then splits, bear right onto a vague path climbing a wooded bank to a wall stile at the top, where there is a fine view across the Leven estuary. As the way is not obvious, your map and compass will help in choosing the correct line.

2   Keep walking in the same direction beyond the stile across an open moor. Your compass will again be useful as, further on, the terrain is sometimes boggy and might require a little experimentation to determine the driest route across. Aim to pass below and to the left of the highest ground ahead, shortly losing height towards a gap in a wall beyond it. Through that, follow the course of a stream, which initially lies to your right but is then crossed lower down at a marker. Keep going in the same direction,

recrossing the waters further on and eventually reaching a gate in the wall lower down. Now, bear left along a grass track, which drops to a roughly metalled way and there, turn right towards a farm at Field End.

3   At the farm, instead of following the track left into the yard, leave it and walk ahead up the edge of a rough pasture. Ignore a ladder stile on the left and continue over the crest to a squeeze stile by the field corner. Now in open woodland, follow the wall on the left for about 20 yards to a second stile, beyond which a path leads down to a gate and out onto a sparsely wooded heath. A vague green track winds on around a boggy area and down to two gates in the corner of the enclosure. Pass through the one ahead and continue along a track towards the farm you can now see, Seatle.

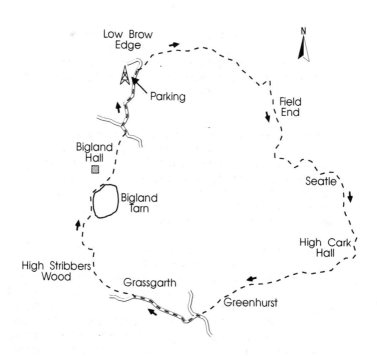

Badgers

If you pass this way at dusk, you might be lucky enough to see a badger in the woods beyond Field End Farm. Although they often favour woodland, badgers are equally at home on the fringes of cultivated areas, seeking cover for their setts below hedges or in small patches of shrubbery. Their principle diet is earthworms, but they will also eat seeds, berries, fruit and occasionally carrion. Prolific tunnellers, badgers are continually extending their burrows and the family group or cete will inhabit the same sett for many generations. Indeed, some still in use have been shown to be over one hundred years old.

Badgers appear to make good neighbours and will occasionally live beside rabbits or even share their holes with a lone fox, an animal that is really quite lazy when it comes to digging out a den.

4   Before you arrive at the farm, climb steps up the banking on the left to a stile, from which a waymark directs the path around the buildings. After passing a large barn, turn right through a gate and then left towards a white farmhouse. There, turn sharp right but then go left between another cottage and barn. Just behind the barn, pass through a gate on the right and on through a second gate to follow a walled track down between fields into the corner of a pasture. Keep going ahead but, approaching the bottom, bear left to find a stile near the corner leading onto an unsurfaced lane. Follow that down to the right, through gates, ultimately emerging onto a tarmac track by High Cark Hall Farm.

5   Turn right and walk through the farm, continuing beyond a gate along a rough track onto the open fellside. After crossing a stream, but before reaching another gate, turn right onto a grass track, but almost at once, leave it to climb a stile in a fence over to the left. With your back to the stile, bear right to pick up a rising field track, which shortly bends and drops to a gate. Immediately through that, leave the obvious track and bear right along a fainter path across the open heath, the route being confirmed by occasional markers. After crossing a fence stile you will shortly reach a wall, where you should turn right, following it to a stile about 40 yards along. Over that, follow the wall on your left down to a gate and out onto a drive

coming from Greenhurst Farm. Walk away from the buildings, to emerge over a cattlegrid onto a lane.

6   Turn right, but almost immediately, go left onto a lesser lane and follow that for about ½ mile to a white house, Grassgarth. Just after it, go through a kissing-gate on the right, waymarked Cumbria Coastal Way, cross a stream by a plank bridge and then follow a wall away from the house. Beyond a gate, a gently climbing path leads through High Stribbers Wood, the sparse trees allowing a grand view across the Leven estuary. Emerging through a gate from the trees, go left along a green trod that then bends right, following a wall towards Bigland Tarn, which shortly comes into view ahead.

7   Go down to the shore and follow it around to the left, shortly passing below Bigland Hall and on along a track at the far end of the lake. When you then reach a junction, bear left, the way being signed to the Riding School, and walk past the stables, eventually emerging from the estate at a road junction. Cross to the road opposite, signed Backbarrow and Newby Bridge, and follow it down, bearing right at a minor junction a little way along, to return to your car.

6

Finsthwaite to Summer House Knott

A pleasant countryside and woodland walk from the little hamlet of Finsthwaite to the top of Summer House Knott, where there is a curious tower and a wonderful view across the head of the River Leven as it leaves Windermere. The walk begins near Stott Park Bobbin Mill and, as the route is relatively short, you could combine it with a visit there to complete the day.

Total distance: 3.1 miles (5km)
Height gain: 540 feet (165m)
Start: High Dam car park, north-east of Finsthwaite, GR SD368882

1   Walk back from the car park to the lane and turn right towards Finsthwaite. Approaching the village, after passing the first cottage on the left, turn left along a narrow lane leading to the church. Continue past the church and former schoolhouse (now the village hall) and through a gate at the end into a field.

St Peter's Church

The church, dedicated to St Peter, is rather distinctive in having a squat, pyramidal topped tower rising from the centre of its roof. It is a comparatively modern building and was completed in 1874, replacing an earlier eighteenth century chapel. The design won an award for its local architects, Paley and Austin, whose work features in many other local churches.

Buried in the churchyard is Clementina Johannes Sobiesky Douglass of Waterside who, some say, was a daughter of Bonnie Prince Charlie. Interestingly in the nineteenth century, two brothers, sons of a naval lieutenant, Thomas Allen, took the name Sobieski, claiming that they were grandchildren of the prince.

2 Follow a track across this and the next field to a stile in the far wall, which leads into a wood. A few yards beyond that, at a junction, turn sharp right onto a lesser path climbing into the trees. It shortly bends left to another fork, where you should take the left branch. Later bear right where another track joins from the left.

3 Where the track eventually crests the hill leave it and go through an opening in a stone wall above to the right, from which an undulating path rises to the left through a more open woodland towards the top of Summer House Knott. Bear left at a junction of tracks near the top and walk on to the tower, which lies hidden in the trees to the left of the path.

The tower was erected as a summerhouse and naval memorial at the end of the eighteenth century. A much-weathered plaque mounted high on the south wall reads:

Erected to honour the officers, seamen and marines of the Royal Navy whose matchless conduct and irresistible valour decisively defeated the fleets of France, Spain and Holland and preserved and protected liberty and commerce.

At present the tower is in a poor state of repair, but there are plans for its restoration and the construction of a viewing platform on the top. However, in the meantime, to enjoy the view from this delightful vantage overlooking Newby Bridge, you must walk on just a little further.

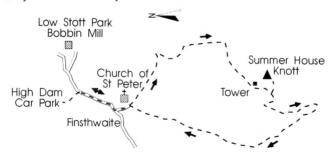

4   Carry on beyond the tower, now gently losing height to pass through a gap in a wall to a junction by a marker post. For the view across the valley, turn left and climb up to a small rocky outcrop overlooking the Leven.

5   Return to the marker, but now walk on past it, the path dropping steeply down steps. In wet weather these can be slippery, so take care with young children. The path continues its descent beyond there, shortly reaching another marker where it bends sharply left. Lower down the hill, beyond a gate, the path then enclosed, drops beside a cottage to end over a stile onto a track.

6   To the right, after passing a few cottages at its end, the track narrows to a woodland path and rises eventually to a stile and gate. Beyond there, bear left at a fork and carry on over the hilltop, where the way passes through a break in a stone wall. A ladder stile further on takes the path out of the trees into a long field.

7   Walk away along its centre, descending through successive fields towards Finsthwaite, which shortly comes into view ahead. Leave the bottom of the final field through a gate, which returns you to the lane in front of the church. Turn left and then right to retrace your steps to the car park at High Dam.

Low Stott Mill

The industrial revolution is commonly associated with the growth of factories in the big towns and cities. However, works also sprang up in quite isolated places, taking advantage of locally available raw materials or a power source. Low Stott Mill was a part of that new age, built in 1835 to produce wooden bobbins for the Lancashire textile mills.

The mill was built here to take advantage of a ready source of coppice wood and power obtained from a dam, constructed on the hillside behind. For 50 years, a 32-foot diameter waterwheel was used to drive the lathes, but a more efficient water turbine, enabling it to produce 10 gross of bobbins every hour later replaced it. At one time there were 64 bobbin mills like this in Lakeland, between them producing 50% of all the bobbins used in the country. Stott Park finally closed in 1971, but is now run by English Heritage as a working museum.

7

Around Middle Dale Plantations

*Although not of any great distance, this forest walk
involves a couple of steady climbs over the higher
ground that separates Dale Park Beck from the low hills
to the east overlooking Windermere. However, the effort
is well repaid by a lovely walk, some of it through oak
woodland, along largely unfrequented paths.*

**Total distance: 4 miles (6.2km)
Height gain: 790 feet (240m)
Start: Woodland car park beside a minor road at Low
Dale. GR SD349917**

1   Turn left from the car park back onto the lane and walk up about
a third of a mile to a house at Middle Dale. Immediately past it,
leave the lane and bear right along a track that rises through a gate
onto a wooded hillside. At the top of the oak wood, pass through
an opening in a stone wall into a conifer plantation and turn left,
continuing to climb beside the wall. After about ¼ mile, the wall
drops away from the path, but keep ahead, following the track
through the plantation. Beyond the crest of the hill, the path
descends through the trees, eventually emerging onto a road.

2   Turn right and walk along it for about two-thirds of a mile, until
you reach Bark Barn Forge at Graythwaite. Immediately beyond
the buildings, turn right onto a marked bridleway that climbs
behind them into the forest.

3   Ignore minor paths and tracks leading off into the trees on
either side as the track climbs up the hillside. Eventually, after it
levels, you will reach a fork where you should continue ahead. The
way then begins to lose height as it follows the base of a deepening

valley. Lower down, the descent steepens and shortly reaches one of the forest lumber roads.

4   Go straight over and pick up the continuation of the path, dropping a short distance through the trees towards a crossing wall. However, just before you reach it, at a junction of paths, turn right to follow a sign indicating the way to Low Dale Park. A clear path, confirmed by occasional markers, winds gently downwards through the trees, shortly passing through a broken wall and eventually leading to a gate out of the forest. Through that, bear right alongside the wall, later joining a field track that leads down to a gate in front of some cottages. Keep going beyond the buildings, but immediately past them, turn left along an enclosed footpath that drops back to the lane opposite the car park at Low Dale Park.

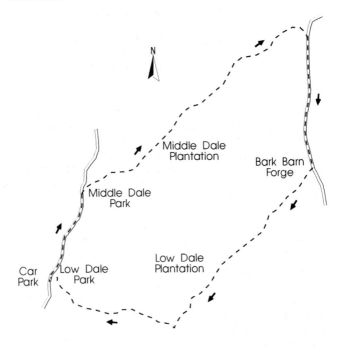

8

Grizedale Forest, Esthwaite and Satterdale

Grizedale is famous for, amongst other things, its forest sculptures. And, although this walk explores some of the plantation's lesser-visited areas, keep your eyes open, for sculptures can be found there too and appear in some of the most unlikely places. See how many you can find and give your imagination free rein in considering what they might represent

Total distance: 7.6 miles (12.2km)
Height gain: 1,150 feet (350m)
Start: Grizedale Forest Visitor Centre. GR SD335944

1   Almost opposite the entrance to the main Visitor Centre car park, a track (indicated by green and white markers) climbs away from the road. Follow it into the forest until, at the top of the climb, you reach a junction with a lumber road. Turn sharp left and walk along it for about 1¼ miles. The way passes through both mature forest and areas recently felled, which, further on, allow a view ahead to Latterbarrow and, in the distance, High Street.

2   Eventually, when you reach a junction, turn left and walk out to the road near Moor Top car park. There, go right, but after only some 50 yards, turn off through a gate and stile on the right to follow a farm track signed to High Barn and Esthwaite Water. After about 350 yards, the track begins to lose height and High Barn Farm comes into view ahead. At that point, turn right off the track and cross a rough pasture to a gate in a deer fence. Through that, bear left on a winding path through an area of new forest, shortly rising to emerge onto a broad forest track. The lake you see, down

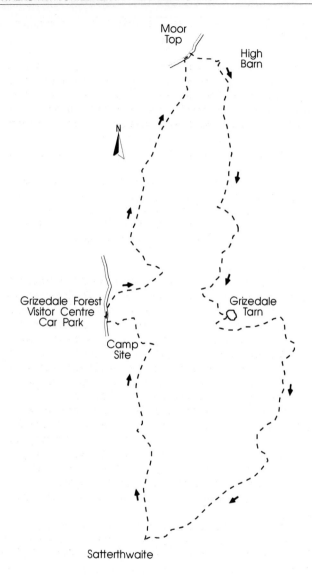

to the left, is Esthwaite Water, and beyond that, the higher ground of Claife Heights.

3   Go left and follow the gradually descending track for about ¼ mile to a sharp left-hand bend. There, leave it, walking ahead on a lesser waymarked track leading through a deer gate. After climbing through mature forest, the way is joined by another track from the left. Bear right and walk on to a wide forest trail at the end, and there turn left. Don't forget to look around you, for even out here, you'll find strange entities lurking in the trees or behind rocks.

4   After a little over ¾ mile, you'll pass an intriguing stone structure in a clearing to the left of the trail. A short distance beyond it, at a green and white marker, turn left off the track and follow a path through the trees, which leads to a viewpoint overlooking Grizedale Tarn, the only natural lake in the whole of the forest.

Grizedale Forest

Although it cannot be described as 'native woodland', Grizedale has remained forested since prehistoric times. The first significant clearings were made by Scandinavian settlers, felling areas in the valleys and on lower slopes for farming and grazing, and indeed the old Norse word for pig is 'griss', describing the valley as a place where pigs were reared. In the eleventh century, the forest was part of the lands managed by Furness Abbey and was extensively exploited for its resources; wood and farming land, a practice that continues to the present day.

Had it been indiscriminately felled, the forest would have very quickly been destroyed, but from early times, it was carefully managed to provide renewable resources. Coppicing, the practice of periodic cutting back to the stump without killing the tree, produced a constant supply of small timber for charcoal production, wood turning and small manufacture, whilst selective felling and replacement of mature trees gave a steady supply of large timber.

Over the centuries, a great many industries sprang up within the forest; charcoal burning, wood turnery, hurdle making, leather tanning, iron smelting and forging, gunpowder production and lime burning to name a few. During the medieval period, its

> *products supported the founding and development of Furness Abbey and closer to our own time, they helped spawn the industrial revolution. Forestry remains important, but today the timber is taken out of the forest to centres of production across the country.*

5   Turn around and walk away from the tarn but then, instead of going right to retrace your steps, walk ahead on another path, which returns you to the main track at a junction just beyond the point where you left it. Go left and follow the main track (identified by green markers) for about 1¼ miles, ignoring lesser tracks and footpaths. Now dropping and having re-entered a mature plantation, look out for a footpath rising from the left and crossing into the forest on the right, marked by a blue post. Note that this is the second path on the right indicated by a blue marker, the first was passed about 250 yards back.

6   After a short climb, the path then falls. Ignore a waymarked path off to the left and carry on ahead until you reach a forest road. Cross straight over along the continuation of the path, still following blue marker posts. Eventually, the path drops out of the plantation into an oak and beech wood and shortly, the houses of Satterthwaite come into view.

7   Just before you reach the first cottage, take a path on the right (still marked as the blue trail) that climbs sharply up the wooded hillside. Later on it levels and, beyond a stile over a broken wall, contours across a steeply sloping wooded hillside. Keep ahead, where the path is later joined by a red trail from the right.

> *Nearby is a restored potash pit, where stone was burnt to produce fertiliser to improve the valley fields. You will notice that it is built into the hillside, a labour saving feature that enabled it to be charged at the top and, after firing, emptied from the bottom.*

8   Beyond there, the track drops steeply to cross a stream and then ends at a wide forest track. Turn left, but after only a few yards, where the track bends sharply left, leave it to follow a path

(indicated by yellow markers) which drops to the right, over a stream and then climbs a wooded bank beyond. Where it forks part way up, bear left, still following yellow markers and carry on to join another forest road.

9   Go left, but after about 40 yards, leave again on the left along a path (marked by yellow and white posts) that drops out of the plantation into mixed woodland. At a junction a few yards on, ignore the path to the left and carry on ahead to another junction. There bear right and keep walking ahead, now following white marker posts. A little further on, where the path again forks, take the climbing right-hand branch, marked blue and white. It gradually rises along a wooded valley before eventually turning to cross a bridge over it.

10 Turn left on the other side and where the path shortly forks, take the higher path on the right, which ultimately ends at Grizedale Hall car park by a campsite. Walk through to the road and you will find the Visitor Centre, just along to the right.

Pheasants

Around many Lakeland woods, you are likely to see or hear pheasants as they strut through the undergrowth. As with many birds, the female is quite drab in comparison to her mate, which helps her disappear into the background when guarding her chicks. By contrast the male is positively gaudy, displaying a bright, colourful plumage. Although a common bird, it is not native to Britain and was introduced from Asia in the eleventh century.

9

Cunsey Beck

*South of Sawrey, the higher forested hills of Claife to the
north give way to a more rolling and open landscape,
where woods and fields alternating above the lakeshore
create ideal walking country. Although of necessity,
some sections of this route are along lanes, they are
generally quiet, but still keep an eye open for passing
traffic.*

Total distance: 5.8 miles (9.3km)
Height gain: 360 feet (110m)
**Start: National Trust car park at Ash Landing, by the
ferry below Far Sawrey. GR SD387954**

1   From the car park, follow the road up the hill towards Far
Sawrey. Footpaths parallel the road, firstly on the right and then on
the left up the hill, but you are forced back onto the carriageway
higher up. Carry on past two junctions to the crest of the hill, where
you will see two cottages on the left. Turn into the entrance of the
second one, from where a footpath leads to a kissing-gate into the
field behind.

2   Walk away from the field corner beside the right-hand wall,
crossing into the adjacent field by another kissing-gate partway
down. Continue to the bottom, cutting the corner to pass through
a gate into the next field to walk past St Peter's Church.

*   ***St Peter's Church***
*   *A gate on the right leads into the churchyard. The church is
    usually open and you may like to have a look inside. Surrounded
    by fields, St Peter's is Sawrey's church. Its opening was
    reported in the Westmorland Gazette of 15 May 1869 and,*

⁂ *according to the account, it was a fine day for the event and the*
⁂ *church was full. After the inaugural service there was a*
⁂ *celebratory luncheon given in the school hall.*

3   Beyond the church, leave the field through a kissing-gate at the bottom to emerge onto a lane. Now, turn left and walk past a couple of cottages to a field gate on the right. Through that, cross a stream and walk ahead up the field, following a path below some trees on the right, to find a gate and stile just left of its top corner. After that, the way continues around the edge of a small plantation and then

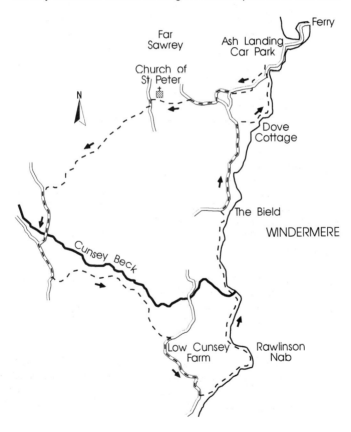

through another field gate. Cross the corner to a second gate and then bear left along the length of that field, finally climbing over a stile into a wood.

4   A winding path continues ahead through the trees, losing height beside a deer fence. At the bottom, join a track from the right and go ahead, passing another track coming from the left to emerge onto a lane. Turn left and walk to its end, where you should again go left. After some 250 yards, at a point where the lane bends right to rise into a wood, cross a stile on the left from which a track is signed to Cunsey Bridge.

5   After skirting the edge of a wood and then fording a stream, the way eventually turns into the trees to run parallel with Cunsey Beck, which lies to the left. Further on, beyond a clearing on the right and a ruined barn, the way forks. Take the right-hand branch into the plantation and, ignoring minor tracks and paths, continue along the main forest track. After cresting a rise, the track falls to end at a lane opposite Low Cunsey Farm.

6   Turn right and follow the lane for about ¼ mile until, immediately before a barn, you will see a path signed across a stile on the left. Take care climbing over, as there is a large drop on the far side, and carry on down to the lake. The path continues northwards along the shore, eventually leading onto a wooded promontory, Rawlinson Nab.

7   Beyond Rawlinson Nab, the path rejoins the water's edge, shortly leading to a bridge under which Cunsey Beck flows into the lake. Walk on past a couple of boat houses, remaining by the lake shore until you are eventually forced to leave the fields over a final stile, emerging onto a lane by a cottage, 'The Bield'.

8   Turn right and follow the lane for about ½ mile, gently gaining height across a wooded bank above the lake. Eventually, at a bend, bear right onto a descending track, signed to Dove Cottage. Beyond the cottage, the way finally rejoins the lakeside. Keep going to the end of the track, which returns to the road opposite the car park at Ash Landing.

10

Moss Eccles Tarn and Claife Heights

After climbing from the ferry to Far Sawrey, this walk leaves the road to explore the open rolling hills on the western flank of Claife Heights. There, you will find a couple of tarns, whose banks make an ideal spot for a picnic. The walk returns through the forest along the top of the hill, where recent felling has, for the time being at any rate, revealed some grand views to the distant mountains.

Total distance: 6.5 miles (10.5km)
Height gain: 980 feet (300m)
Start: National Trust car park at Ash Landing, by the ferry below Far Sawrey. GR SD387954

1   Footpaths, first on the right and then on the left enable you to avoid some of the road walking as you climb away from the car park towards Near Sawrey. Rejoining the road, higher up, carry on past a junction to a point where it bends left. At that point, go through a gate opening on the right, following a track signed to Far and Near Sawrey. When you reach the junction at the top, go ahead through a kissing-gate and continue climbing along the edge of a field, finally leaving through another gate onto a tarmac drive. Follow the drive for about 20 yards towards a house, but where it then bends left, leave it to walk ahead past the front of the house. Through a kissing-gate just beyond, a track returns you to the road by the Sawrey Hotel.

2   Turn right, but after about 50 yards, leave along a minor lane on the right, signed as a bridleway to Moss Eccles Tarn and Claife

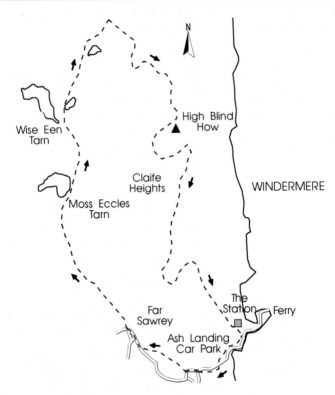

Heights which, having passed some houses, crosses a cattlegrid into an open pasture. About 100 yards further on, where it then bends right, fork left onto a gravel track signed to 'Hawkshead'. After fording a shallow stream the way rises gently through a gate and is later joined by a track coming from the left. Keep going along the main track which, higher up, passes through another gate. You will soon reach some rocky slabs, beyond which Moss Eccles Tarn is suddenly revealed.

3   Continue beyond the lake, bearing left where the track later forks. After another gate, Wise Een Tarn comes into view ahead, the track passing to the right of it below a small reservoir. Beyond

the tarns, the track turns towards the forest and, after passing through another gate, leads into the trees.

4   At a fork, bear right, after which the track winds downwards, shortly reaching a junction, where the main track bends left. Leave there, turning right onto a path signed 'Ferry and Far Sawrey'. Occasional white-topped posts mark the twisting path through the trees, eventually leading you to another signpost. Go right there and, after initially following a wall, bear left and climb over the summit of the hill. Recent felling has opened up the views, which for a while, will remain quite spectacular.

Forestry Commission

It was during the First World War that the country's dependence upon imported timber was first realised and the post-war years saw the creation of the Forestry Commission and the establishment of commercial forests throughout the country. Softwood varieties such as Sitka spruce, larch and pines mature quickly and do relatively well on the often-poor soils of Britain's northern hills and were used extensively as the basis of the plantations.

Many areas of the forest are now reaching maturity and, just like any other crop, are being harvested. The cleared areas will then be replanted or, in some cases, allowed to regenerate but in the meantime, taking advantage of the open space, small woodland plants and flowers exert their own position, bringing a splash of colour and new variety to the landscape.

5   Beyond the top, the way bends to the right, losing height to reach a forest road. Turn right, but after only a short distance, beyond a small mossy tarn, turn left onto a narrow path, signed 'Far Sawrey and Ferry'. Occasional markers confirm the way, which, after a while, passes below a rocky outcrop at High Blind How. There is another fine view if you detour to its summit.

6   Carry on along the path, which shortly crosses a small stream and later, leads by some rocks, where the way to Sawrey Ferry is again confirmed. Further on, yet another marker directs you left by a rocky slab, below which the path drops back into the wood,

eventually ending at a junction with a more prominent track. Turn right, still following signs to Far Sawrey, but break your walk a few yards on to visit yet another viewpoint. Overlooking Windermere and Belle Isle, it is reached through a gap in a wall through the trees on the left.

7 Continue along the track, which after passing through a couple of gates, leaves the forest and drops to a junction. There, turn left, signed to Windermere, Lake Shore and Ferry, and follow the track through another gate, until you arrive at a kissing-gate on the right. Through that and signed 'The Ferry', a path passes through intermittent woodland before turning to drop down a steep wooded hillside. Eventually, the way passes through a rocky cleft to a ruined folly, known as The Station. Go under its archway and turn down a stepped pathway, turning right at the bottom to return to the car park.

Windermere

Some 10½ miles long and, at its widest, almost a mile across, Windermere is the largest of Cumbria's lakes and the most popular for water sport enthusiasts. From antiquity, it was a thoroughfare, providing a direct water passage into the heart of the area. But the fashion for pleasure cruises evolved during the Victorian period, when rich industrialists whiled away their leisure hours on luxurious steamers and elegant yachts, sailing from moorings below their grand houses built around the shores. Today's sailors are often more intent on sport, but you can still cruise the lake in style on a nineteenth-century steamer.